AF241480

God the Great Conductor

Orchestrating Every Aspect of My Life

Romans 8:28

ABOUT THE AUTHOR

The author, Yolanda Lance is a woman of faith who believes deeply in God's ability to transform broken moments into beautiful purpose. Through teaching, writing, and creative expression, she is passionate about helping other to grow spiritually, trust God more fully, and recognize His hand at work in their everyday lives.

Her heart is to encourage women to see that God is always present, guiding, shaping, and orchestrating each season with intention and love. This book was created as a sacred space for reflection, healing, and renewed faith.

Dedicated to those
who believe that
"all things work
together for good"
(Romans 8:28), even
when the journey is
difficult.

Table of Contents

 1. Joseph Goes from a Pit to a Palace (Gen. 37-50) Page 8

 2. Positioned on Purpose" (Esther 1–10) Page 12

 3. Loss Turned into Legacy (Book of Ruth) Page 15

 4.Delayed But Delivered (Exodus 1–14) Page 18

 5. Tears That Gave Birth Purpose (1 Samuel 1–2) Page 20

 6. A Quiet Yes That Changed Everything (Luke 1–2) Page 22

 7. When God Restores What Life Took (Ruth) Page 24

 8. When God Interrupts Your Plans (Acts 9)Page 26

 9. When Waiting Meets Wonder (Genesis 12–21) Page 28

 10. It Is Finished: When Love Has the Final Word (Luke 22–24) Page 30

Introduction
God, the Great Conductor

What if nothing in your life has been random? Every delay, detour, and disappointment may be part of a divine design. Like a conductor guiding an orchestra, God orchestrates each moment with intention, bringing harmony even from seasons that feel out of rhythm. Some moments are triumphant; others are quiet and painful, but the Conductor never loses control of the score.

This book invites you to view your life through heaven's lens. From betrayal to blessing and loss to restoration, God remains faithful. Romans 8:28 reminds us that God works all things together for good for those who love Him and are called according to His purpose. Through the stories of women and men shaped by divine orchestration, you are encouraged to pause, trust God's timing, surrender control, and recognize His hand at work in your life.

Chapter 1
Joseph Goes from a Pit to a Palace (Gen. 37-50)

Joseph's life sounds like an all too relatable story that many women and young ladies, including myself either live quietly or out loud. Joseph was betrayed by people he trusted, seasons in his life may have been spent waiting, dealing with situations that may have felt unjust and unfair, and setbacks that may have seemed to negate or erase the promises God had spoken over his life. How many of you can relate to those feelings?

Joseph's journey begins with betrayal. His own brothers, those who were supposed to protect him, to love him, yet they sold him into slavery. For many today, betrayal doesn't always come from enemies; it comes from family, friends, coworkers, or people we have loved and supported. It appeared that the worse form of betrayal can come from those that are closest to you. The pain of being misunderstood, rejected, or discarded can feel like being thrown into a pit with no explanation at all. But guess what, the pit was not Joseph's final destination.

Even though he was wrongfully enslaved, Joseph didn't lose his sense of personal integrity or his work ethic. Joseph was assigned to work in Potiphar's house, after being sold into slavery by his brothers. However, he showed excellence in a system designed to strip him of dignity and self-pride.

Many women and young women in 2025 can relate to being employed and working hard in spaces where they are overlooked, undervalued, or forced to prove themselves repeatedly. Yet Scripture shows us something powerful: God's presence does not disappear when our positions in life change. God was with Joseph in slavery, just as He is with those who find themselves navigating difficult jobs, broken relationships, or financial struggles today.

It didn't end for joseph with being sold into slavery, then came prison. Joseph was falsely accused and punished for doing the "right thing."

This season might speak deeply to those individuals who have felt they have been misunderstood, blamed, or silenced in some shape or form. The sense of being in prison could represent or be equal to those moments when you followed God, yet everything still fell apart. When your obedience didn't bring immediate relief, or even felt like things got worse.

When it felt like doing the right thing cost you everything, and benefitted you in no way. And yet, even in prison, God was working behind the scenes positioning Joseph for future greatness. What looked like a delay was actually divine preparation. As a result of what he had experienced, Joseph learned leadership, wisdom, and discernment behind closed doors. God used the place of confinement to connect Joseph to the very people who would later open the door to the palace for him.

Sometimes what feels like being "stuck" is actually God arranging and orchestrating your next steps. When he was in the right position, Joseph's promotion came suddenly. One day he was a forgotten prisoner; the next, he stood before King Pharaoh as a leader over Egypt. God didn't just elevate Joseph for his own benefit, but He promoted Joseph so that entire nations would be saved during a famine through him. What others meant for harm became the very path God used to preserve life.

This is where Joseph's story becomes deeply personal for women today. Every setback, every betrayal, delay, and painful season…was not wasted. God used it all to shape Joseph into someone strong enough, wise enough, and compassionate enough to carry responsibilities that would be place upon him, and receive the blessings that were designed specifically for him.

Joseph later said to his brothers:
"You intended to harm me, but God intended it for good…" (Genesis 50:20). In modern terms, Joseph was saying: What broke me didn't break God's plan. What hurt me didn't cancel the purpose for my life.

For women in 2025 and beyond, Joseph's story reminds us that:
- The pit does not define your future
- The prison does not cancel God's promises
- Delays are not denials
- God is always working behind the scenes

God is still the Great Conductor, weaving together every painful note, every pause, and every unexpected turn into something purposeful. What feels like loss today may be the very thing God is using to position you to bless others tomorrow. Your story, like Joseph's, is still being written. And God has not forgotten you…

Something To Think About:
What painful season in your life might God be using as preparation rather than punishment?

Chapter 2
Positioned on Purpose

Esther's story reminds us of that God often positions us long before we understand why. Esther didn't step into the palace knowing a crisis was on the way. She simply said yes to the process, that meant trusting God even when the purpose wasn't clear yet.

Esther was an ordinary young woman, no special attributes according to society, however, she had an extraordinary assignment that not even she could see at first. She was an orphan, raised by her cousin Mordecai, living under foreign rule. Nothing about her early life suggested that she was royalty. Many women and young ladies today can relate to feeling unseen, overlooked, or unsure if their lives really matter, or are important to the bigger picture.

Then came the royal search for a new queen. To modern readers, the concept of a beauty contest may sound uncomfortable or superficial, but in Esther's world, it was the door God used to move her into a position. What others saw as appearance, God saw as access. At times, people allow outward appearance, physical beauty, position, and status in life to influence how they judge others. However, God used what others view, to form a strategic move to place Esther in a position to acquire a seat on the throne. Esther didn't chase the throne; she was chosen for it.

Sometimes opportunities come through unexpected or even confusing paths. God can use doors that don't look spiritual to accomplish deeply spiritual purposes. Esther found favor, not just because of her beauty, but because God's hand was on her life. Favor placed her in rooms she didn't qualify for on paper.

Have you ever experienced seeing people or even you may have found yourself place in a position that others may feel that you should not have been chosen for. I've heard people say favor doesn't seem fair, however when God is attached to it, it is attached to purpose, and it is just.

Many women today experience this kind of favor, being selected, promoted, or given influence without fully understanding why. Favor is not luck; it's God quietly arranging outcomes behind the scenes. What's powerful about Esther's story is timing. God placed her in the palace before the threat against the Jewish people was announced. She didn't rise during the crisis, she was already positioned when it came. In the same way,

God often prepares us ahead of time, and that can be through education, relationships with others, skills, and experiences, commonly long before we realize why we need them. When the crisis finally came, Esther faced fear, risk, and uncertainty. By speaking up, she risked losing her life. Silence felt safer, but obedience mattered more. Mordecai's words still echo today: "And who knows but that you have come to your royal position for such a time as this?" (Esther 4:14) In modern terms, he was saying: You didn't get here by accident. Your influence, your voice, your access, none of it is random.

For women and young ladies in 2025, Esther's story reminds us that:

- God can use your position, no matter how small it may feel to you or others
- Preparation often happens in ordinary seasons of life
- Courage is choosing to be obedient, even when fear or anxiety is present
- Silence can cost more than speaking up

Esther didn't save a nation because she was fearless. She did it because she trusted God enough to act despite her fear. Her obedience released deliverance not just for herself, but for generations to come. You may not wear a crown, but you do carry influence, in your home, school, workplace, church, or community. God has placed you where you are on purpose, with a voice that matters.
So, when life asks more of you than you feel ready to give, remember Esther. You are not behind. You are not overlooked. You are positioned, for such a time as this.

Something To Think About:
Where has God positioned me that I may not fully understand yet?

Chapter 3
Loss Turned into Legacy

The book of Ruth is a powerful reminder that God is the Great Orchestrator, working through seasons of loss, uncertainty, and quiet obedience to produce a legacy far greater than we can imagine.

Ruth's story begins with famine, a season of lack that forced Naomi's family to leave Bethlehem in search of survival. For Ruth, this wasn't a journey that she chose, it was a disruption of events in her life. How many of you can relate to unexpected and sometimes unwanted seasons of financial strain, job loss, displacement, broken relationships, or even dreams put on hold. Yet even the moment of famine was part of God's orchestration for Ruth. What looked like deprivation was positioning, which was a prompt that moved Ruth toward the place where her destiny would unfold.

Ruth experienced deep grief. She lost her husband, her security, and her future as she knew it. As a young widow in a foreign land, she had every reason to return to what was familiar, what was in her eyes comfortable.

Many women today know, can relate to, and completely understand this kind of grief, losing a spouse, a parent, a child, a relationship, or even the life they thought they would have. I can personally understand this, in my early 20's I had my life all planned out perfectly. And now in my 50's, nothing has gone exactly how I thought it would, but to God be the glory, I am blessed and I am able to see HIS hand throughout my entire life. Like many in grief, Ruth's pain was real, but it was not wasted. God did not rush her through grief; He walked with her through it, because healing can be a process. Ultimately God was preparing her heart for what was ahead.

Ruth's defining moment came when she chose loyalty and obedience over comfort. Her words to Naomi, "Where you go, I will go," were not emotional promises but covenant-level commitment. She chose to walk in faith without knowing the outcome. In today's world, obedience often looks like staying faithful when no one is watching, continuing to serve when you feel unseen, and trusting God when the plan is unclear. Ruth didn't obey for a reward, she obeyed because she trusted God.

What should be understood about Ruth, she didn't chase greatness; she showed up faithfully. She worked in the fields, gleaning what others left behind. That's where God's favor met her. Boaz noticed her, not because she demanded or sought attention, but because God highlighted her obedience. Redemption came through divine alignment. Boaz became her kinsman-redeemer, restoring her dignity, security, and future. This reminds us that God often redeems our lives through quiet faithfulness, not public applause.

Ruth's story did not end with survival, it ended

with an establishment of legacy. This Moabite woman, once an outsider, became the great-grandmother of King David and part of the lineage of Jesus Christ. When the world labeled her as, foreign, widowed, disadvantaged, God redefined her as chosen, redeemed, and essential. Her life proves that your past does not disqualify you from God's promises.

Every detail of Ruth's story, famine, loss, obedience, redemption, was woven together by God's hand. What seemed random was intentional. What felt painful was purposeful. Ruth did not see the full picture like many of us, but God did. This is why Boaz could say to her: "The Lord repay you for what you have done, and a full reward be given you by the Lord, the God of Israel, under whose wings you have come to take refuge." Ruth 2:12 For the women and young ladies who feel overlooked, exhausted, or uncertain, Ruth's story speaks hope.

God sees your faithfulness. He honors your obedience. He redeems aspects of your loss. And He specializes in turning broken beginnings into eternal legacies. What feels like loss today may be the very thing God is using to position you for a future you cannot yet imagine. Trust the Orchestrator. Your story is still unfolding.

Something To Think About:
How might God be using your faithfulness in small choices to shape a bigger story?

Chapter 4
Delayed But Delivered

Moses' life reminds us that delays are not denials when God is orchestrating the story. From the very beginning, God was quietly at work, guiding, protecting, and preparing Moses long before Moses understood the purpose God had for his life.

Moses was born into danger as a Hebrew under oppression, yet God placed him in safety by having him adopted into Pharaoh's household. What looked like a contradiction was actually divine preparation. God allowed Moses to grow up learning leadership, order, and authority in Egypt, while never removing his connection to Hebrew suffering. I don't know about you, but I can definitely relate to the feeling of being caught between two worlds of past pain and future purpose, yet without understanding why.

After he fled Egypt because of a "situation" (Exodus 2:11–15), Moses spent years in exile tending sheep. This season felt like a setback to Moses, but it was a sacred pause. God was shaping his heart through humility, patience, and quiet dependence. For those seasons when life slows down, dreams feel distant, or progress seems stalled, Moses' story reassures us that God often does His deepest work in hidden places.

God places a calling on Moses' life not while he was in a palace, but while he was in the wilderness. At the burning bush, Moses felt inadequate and afraid, but God's response was simple and comforting: "I will be with you." (Exodus 3:12). God did not promise ease; He promised presence. Just as Moses was, many women may know the feelings of being unprepared or unsure, yet God calls them anyway, offering His steady guidance and companionship.

God used every part of Moses' journey, his Hebrew roots, Egyptian training, and wilderness waiting, to eventually deliver His people. Moses understood oppression because he had seen it, and leadership because he had experienced it. Nothing was wasted. God orchestrated every delay into preparation for deliverance.

Moses' life reminds us that God's timing is intentional. If your journey feels delayed, know that God is still with you, still shaping you, and still preparing you for what's ahead. The same God who walked with Moses walks with you, faithfully orchestrating every step.

Something To Think About:
What part of my past may God be using as training for my calling?

Chapter 5
Tears That Gave Birth Purpose

Hannah's life gently reminds us that God sees every tear we shed and weaves even our deepest pain into His greater plan. Her story shows how God, the Great Orchestrator, works quietly
through sorrow, prayer, and promise to bring forth His purpose in our lives.

Hannah carried the heavy ache of barrenness, she was unable to have children, even though she deeply desired to be a mother. This caused her great sorrow and made her feel overlooked and misunderstood. Her barrenness caused her to turn to God in prayer, and where God in turn later revealed to her His power and purpose in her life. Your "barrenness" does not necessarily have to be pregnancy, it could pertain to a strong desire for something, like a relationship, a good job, a close friend, a vehicle, a better life situation, etc. God never looked away from the circumstances that Hannah faced.

Instead of allowing bitterness and resentment to take root in her heart and mind, Hannah brought her broken heart to God. Her prayers were raw and honest, offered with tears rather than perfect words. I admire people who are completely honest with God. It may seem obvious, but being real with Him makes sense, He already knows our deepest thoughts and feelings. In her surrender, Hannah trusted God with the one thing she longed for most.

This is a gentle reminder that God welcomes our honest prayers and hears us even when our voices tremble.

When God responded, Hannah held her promise with open hands. She understood that the blessing was not meant to end with her. Her obedience revealed deep faith, she trusted the Orchestrator with both her pain and her miracle.

Hannah's tears gave birth to her son Samuel, a prophet who would shape the future of a nation by anointing kings. Her private prayers produced public purpose. What began as personal sorrow became a legacy that touched generations. .

According to 1 Samuel 1:19, God heard Hannah's and remembered her. We are not forgotten by God. For every woman who has cried silent tears or carried unseen pain, gain comfort and hope from Hannah's story. Trust and know that God remembers you. He is faithfully orchestrating every season, turning barrenness into blessing, prayer into promise, and tears into purpose.

Something To Think About:

What prayer have you been pouring out that I need to trust God's timing with?

Chapter 6
A Quiet Yes That Changed Everything (Luke 1–2)

Mary's story reminds us that God, the Great Orchestrator, often works through quiet lives and willing hearts. She was young, unknown, and lived what some might consider an ordinary life, when heaven interrupted her plans. God did not choose Mary for her status or position, but for her humility and faith. When the angel announced God's divine assignment, Mary faced uncertainty, risk, and misunderstanding. Yet she responded not with fear, but with surrender. Her words, "May your word to me be fulfilled" (Luke 1:38), was a declaration of trust in God's greater plan.

Understand that this may seem easier said than done for some. Well, I can only speak for myself. I would like to think that I would have submitted easily, but in reality, knowing me, I probably would have said something like, "uhhhhhhhh God are you sure" or say to myself, "that's my mind talking to me, that's not God." That kind of surrender is to be celebrated. However, Mary's obedience was not loud or celebrated, it was faithful. She carried the promise of God through unseen moments, and that were clearly behind closed doors, as they are not documented in scripture in full detail. In Luke 1:29, we see that she experienced some confusion at the message that was sent to her by the angel. Also, in Luke 1:34, she did have sincere questions of what would take place in her life, yet she decided to trust that He who called her would also sustain her. The world may have overlooked her, God positioned her at the center of His redemptive plan. Though Mary faced uncertainty, fear of the possibility of being misunderstood, and feeling unprepared to carry the weight of responsibility that was placed upon her, she decided to trust God with this divine assignment that changed history. Through Mary's yes, our Savior entered the world. Her story gently reminds us that God can take a willing heart and weave it into something eternal.

When we surrender to God's orchestration, even our quiet obedience can change history. If you are one of those that carry hidden burdens, unexpected responsibilities, or callings you've never planned for, please understand that Mary's life reminds us that God does not wait for perfection, He looks for a willingness of the heart and mind.

Her obedience did not remove the challenges, but it invited God's presence into every step. The world may overlook your faithfulness, God sees it. In the same manner that God orchestrated every detail of Mary's journey, He is carefully guiding yours. Your yes, spoken in prayer, patience, or perseverance, may be part of a greater story than you can see right now. Trust the Orchestrator. Hope is being formed, even in the unseen.

Something To Think About:

Am I willing to say yes to God even when the plan stretches me?

Chapter 7
When God Restores What Life Took

Naomi's story is for every woman who has ever whispered, "Lord, this is not how I imagined my life would turn out." She knew loss deeply, famine, the death of her husband, and the loss of both sons. Her heart was so heavy that she told people to call her Mara, meaning bitter. Let's be honest, some seasons in our life are so rough, that we could easily earn the name Mara. Yet even in Naomi's heartbreak, God was still orchestrating behind the scenes. What felt like an ending was actually a turning point in her life.

When Naomi returned to Bethlehem, from the land of Moab, she came back empty-handed, or so it seemed. She had no plan, no resources, and no emotional energy left to fake any glimpse of optimism or hope. But… she did have Ruth, a loyal daughter-in-law whose obedience would become part of God's restoration plan for her. Sometimes God's provision doesn't show up as a miracle in the blink of an eye, it shows up as a person who refuses to leave your side or support that is unwavering.

Through Ruth's faithfulness and Boaz's kindness, God quietly began rebuilding Naomi's life. Boaz wasn't just generous, he was intentional. God used everyday obedience and simple acts of kindness to restore what grief and heartache had stolen. Naomi went from coaching Ruth in survival mode to holding a grandchild in her arms. Talk about a plot twist.

When the women of the town declared, "The Lord has not left you without a guardian-redeemer" (Ruth 4:14), it was a reminder that God had never abandoned Naomi, even when she felt forgotten. Naomi's life reminds modern women that God can restore joy after loss, purpose after pain, and laughter after bitterness.

If you're in a season where your faith feels tired and your patience is on backorder, take heart. God is still orchestrating. He may not be finished with your story, and He's definitely not done blessing you.

Something To Think About:
Where might God be restoring joy in areas I thought were permanently broken?

Chapter 8
When God Interrupts Your Plans (Acts 9)

Paul's story is proof that God can and does interrupt a life headed in the wrong direction and turn it into something extraordinary. Before he was Paul, he was Saul, confident, driven, and completely convinced he was right… while like some today, doing all the wrong things. He was actively and intentionally persecuting believers, certain he was serving God, God stepped in and put a halt to his actions. That was absolutely not going to continue on God's watch.

On the road to Damascus, God orchestrated a divine interruption that literally knocked Saul off his feet and blinded him. Sometimes God gets our attention in what we might consider very dramatic ways, because we don't often take subtle hints. This moment wasn't punishment; it was redirection. God met Saul in the middle of his mess and rewrote his story.

Saul went from a feared persecutor to faithful servant amongst those around him. The same passion that he once used to tear the church down, God redirected to build it up. When God said, "This man is my chosen instrument" (Acts 9:15).God made it clear that Saul's past was not a disqualifier for him to be used by God, it prepared him to be used by God.

God orchestrated every part of Paul's life, his education, his bold personality, even his mistakes, for an even greater purpose. Absolutely nothing was wasted. What looked like a total spiritual plot twist was actually a "divine setup".

For the woman who feels like she's taken a few wrong turns, or maybe a full detour from God's plan for their life, Paul's story serves as a reminder that God specializes in course correction. He can take your past, your personality, and even your stubborn streak, and turn it into purpose. If God could transform Saul into Paul, imagine what He can do with you. Trust the Orchestrator, He's not finished yet.

Something To Think About:

How has God redirected my life in ways I did not expect but now see His hand?

Chapter 9
When Waiting Meets Wonder

Sarah's story is for every woman who has ever checked the calendar, peeped out of a window through the blinds, sighed deeply, sat tapping her feet, and wondered if God's promise somehow got lost in the mail. Please know that from the beginning, God is orchestrating her life, even when the timeline is confusing and doesn't make sense to her.

God promised Sarah a child, but the waiting stretched on... and on...and on. Years passed, birthdays piled up, and hope felt harder to hold on to. Sarah did what many of us do, and I hate to admit it, have done in my life, she tried to help God out a little. Why oh why, do we as mere mortals feel like God could use some assistance from us to fulfill His plans and promises... However, her doubt didn't cancel God's plan, but it did reveal her very human struggle with waiting.

When Sarah overheard it being said that she would have a son in Genesis 18:9–14, she laughed. I wonder if it was a deep belly laugh, bah haaaaaaaaaaaa. She didn't laugh because it was necessarily funny, but because it felt impossible in her mid. Yet God gently asked, "Is there anything too hard for the Lord?" (Genesis 18:14). It wasn't a rebuke; it was a reminder. God's promises are not limited by our age, timing, or circumstances.

At just the right time, God fulfilled His promise. Sarah gave birth to Isaac, whose name actually means laughter. The very thing she once laughed at in disbelief, probably mixed with a little or a lot of doubt, became a source of joy. God turned her waiting into wonder and her doubt into delight.

Sarah's life reminds modern women that delays are NOT denials, doubts don't disqualify us, and God's timing is always intentional. If you're waiting on something that feels long overdue, take heart my friend. The Great Orchestrator is still at work, and nothing is too hard for the Lord.

Something To Think About:
What promise am I still waiting on God to fulfill?

Chapter 10
It Is Finished: When Love Has the Final Word

As this journey comes to a close, we look to Jesus, the ultimate proof that God is not only a great orchestrator, but the perfect one. In Luke 22–24, we see a story that looks like heartbreak, betrayal, and loss... yet is actually the greatest victory ever written.

Jesus was betrayed by someone close, abandoned by friends, falsely accused, and led to the cross. From the outside, it might have looked like failure. Like one more story where love lost and injustice won. Like me many women know and can relate to that feeling, when trust is broken, prayers feel unanswered, and hope seems painfully quiet.

But... God was still orchestrating. The cross was not an interruption to God's plan, it was the plan. What looked like defeat was divine fulfillment. Every tear, every wound, every step toward Calvary was purposeful. And when Jesus declared,
"It is finished." (John 19:30). He wasn't saying "I am done." He was saying "The work is complete."

The weight of sin, shame, fear, and failure was fully carried, and fully conquered. Then came the resurrection. The stone was rolled away, not so Jesus could get out, but so the world could see in. Death did not get the final word. Love did. Victory did. God did.

For the woman who feels worn down, overlooked,

or stuck in a Freaky Friday kind of season, just know, Sunday is coming. What feels like an ending may actually be a beginning. God specializes in turning graves into gardens and heartbreak into hope.

If you've never trusted Jesus, today is the day to re-think your views. All you have to do is invite Him in, believe that He died, rose again, and declare Him as your Savior. In Christ, your story of loss, fear, or doubt can become a story of hope, redemption, and eternal victory. Let God orchestrate your life. God hears and can carry your burdens, forgive your sins, and give you eternal life. Trust the Ultimate Orchestrator. The story isn't over, and in Him, victory is already written.

Something To Think About:
How might God be using something painful
in my life to bring about redemption?

Understand and know,
God is not reacting,
He is conducting.
Every pause, every pain,
every person, and every promise
fits into His divine rhythm.
"And we know that in all things
God works for the good of
those who love Him..."
Romans 8:28